REDNECK WORDS OF WISDOM

RWW

REDNECK WORDS OF WISDOM

REDNECK WORDS ✶✶✶ *of* ✶✶✶ WISDOM

REAL-LIFE EXPRESSIONS, ADVICE, COMMENTARY, AND OBSERVATIONS FROM SOME OF THE SMARTEST PEOPLE AROUND...REDNECKS

COLLECTED BY JAIMIE MUEHLHAUSEN

CHRONICLE BOOKS
SAN FRANCISCO

The redneck words of wisdom compiled in this book have all been collected from rednecks throughout the world at redneckwordsofwisdom.com. All sayings were submitted with permission from the rednecks themselves. Every effort has been made to trace the ownership of any copyrighted material included in this volume. Any errors that may have occurred are inadvertent and will be corrected in subsequent editions, provided notification is sent to the publisher.

Library of Congress Cataloging-in-Publication Data available.

ISBN-13: 978-0-8118-5555-6

Manufactured in China

Book and cover design by Jaimie Muehlhausen/Contusion Design

10 9 8 7 6 5 4 3 2

Chronicle Books LLC
680 Second Street
San Francisco, California 94107
www.chroniclebooks.com

To my wife, Jessica
my favorite redneck

CONTE

NTS

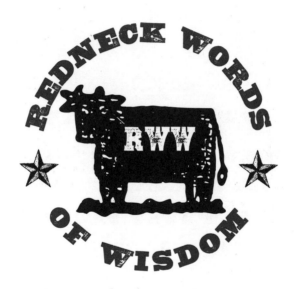

INTRODUCTION

Rednecks are not just from the South. Some of the biggest rednecks I've ever met are from California, Oregon, the Midwest, the Northeast—you name it. In other words, "redneck" is not regional. It's internal. You're either a redneck or you know one.

The best thing about rednecks is their way of expressing themselves. The idea for this book came about when I was visiting relatives in South Carolina. There was a party (isn't there always?), and the next morning I saw one particular in-law looking very hungover. I asked him how he was feeling and he replied:

> ## "I FEEL LIKE I GOT EAT BY A BEAR AND SHIT OFF A CLIFF."

Like I said, rednecks have a way with words. That very relative must have spouted a million of 'em throughout the weekend, not trying to be funny—that's just how he talks.

This collection has been compiled from rednecks all over the world who have submitted their favorite redneck sayings to www.redneckwordsofwisdom.com. They're funny, cutting, and usually right on the money. I hope this book will be of great value to you in your everyday life, as you tap in to your inner redneck. But, like my Great-Uncle Willie used to say, "It's not what it's worth, it's what it'll bring."

So, this book is dedicated to Uncle Willie Eden, Scott Berry, and rednecks around the world to whom these aren't "sayings" at all. It's just the way they talk.

— Jaimie Muehlhausen

09

FUCIUS

EDNECK

YOU PLANT A TATER, YOU GET A TATER.

Never get into an argument with an idiot— you'll just lower yourself to their level and they'll beat you with experience.

Life is simpler when you plow around the stump.

Words that soak into your ears are whispered—not yelled.

IF AT FIRST YOU DON'T SUCCEED, USE DUCT TAPE.

FORGIVE YOUR ENEMIES. IT MESSES UP THEIR HEADS.

Never try to teach a pig how to dance. You'll waste your time and just annoy the pig.

It don't take a very big person to carry a grudge.

YOU CAN'T UNSAY A CRUEL WORD.

Every path has a few puddles.

The best sermons are lived, not preached.

REMEMBER THAT SILENCE IS SOMETIMES THE BEST ANSWER.

When you find yourself in a hole—quit diggin'.

You got to be 10 percent smarter than the equipment you're runnin'.

⬦

Procrastination is like masturbation: it's fun until you realize you just fucked yourself.

⬦

Never get into a wrestlin' match with a pig. You're both gonna get muddy, and chances are, the pig likes it.

⬦

TWO CAN LIVE AS CHEAP AS ONE IF ONE DON'T EAT.

Never lay an angry hand on a kid or an animal. It just ain't helpful.

To know how country folks are doing, look at their barns, not their houses.

Tell me what you need and I'll tell you how to get along without it.

HARD SAYIN' NOT KNOWIN'.

Don't interfere with somethin' that
ain't botherin' you none.

TEACHERS, BANKERS, AND HOOT OWLS SLEEP WITH ONE EYE OPEN.

Good Lord willin' and the creek don't rise.

I can tell you a thing or two
'bout a thing or two.

SOME FRIE

NDLY
ADVICE

Go for the ugly early and you'll never go home alone.

DON'T JUDGE FOLKS BY THEIR RELATIVES.

Don't sell your mule to buy a plow.

Spit in one hand and wish in the other and see which one fills up faster.

KEEP SKUNKS AND BANKERS AT A DISTANCE.

Anyone can fly. It's the landing that will get you.

When you wallow with pigs, expect to get dirty.

If you can't race it or take it to bed, you don't need it.

Most of the stuff people worry about ain't never gonna happen anyway.

Don't name a pig you plan to eat.

We service what we sell, 'cause what we sell needs service.

THAT'LL GO OVER LIKE A PREGNANT POLE VAULTER.

A blow job from a pig is better than a goodnight kiss from a fox.

DON'T SKINNY-DIP WITH SNAPPING TURTLES.

If you want sympathy, look between *shit* and *syphilis* in the dictionary.

There's more ways to choke a dog than feeding him peanut butter.

NO MATTER WHAT YOU DO TO A SKUNK, IT STILL STINKS.

★ ★ ★ ★ ★ ★ ★

JUST CALL ME BUTTER 'CAUSE I'M ON A ROLL.

★ ★ ★ ★ ★ ★ ★

IF I WAS ANY BETTER,  I'D HAVE TO BE TWINS.

★ ★ ★ ★ ★ ★ ★

I AIN'T SCARED OF NOTHIN' BUT SPIDERS AND DRY COUNTIES.

★ ★ ★ ★ ★ ★ ★

About as hard as tryin' to herd chickens.

He's kind of like a billy goat: hard head and stinkin' ass.

Tall enough to stand flat–footed and kiss a giraffe.

Let's be off like a herd of turtles.

We were so poor that we used to have to jerk off the dogs just to feed the cats.

ABOUT AS MUCH FUN AS A WARM BUCKET OF CALF SLOBBER.

He's just like a catfish:
all mouth and no ass.

About as sexy as socks
on a billy goat.

THAT FITS TIGHTER THAN SOCKS ON A ROOSTER.

That's how the cow ate the cabbage.

He's the kind of guy who'll put a rattlesnake in your pocket and ask you for a light.

I'M GONNA GET IT DONE IF IT HARELIPS EVERY COW IN TEXAS.

THEIR TRAILER WAS SO BAD, THERE WAS ROACHES BIG ENOUGH TO STAND FLAT-FOOTED AND SCREW A TURKEY BUZZARD.

A leopard can't change his spots any more than a Z-car its racing stripes.

It's gonna be a frog choker. (a heavy rain)

You mess with the bull, you get the horns.

HE LET HIS ALLIGATOR MOUTH GET AHEAD OF HIS HUMMINGBIRD ASS.

You're worse than a pet raccoon— can't keep your hands off anything.

Faster than a jackrabbit on moonshine.

I'm just a squirrel in the world trying to get a nut.

That boy smells so bad, he could drive a hungry dog off a meat wagon.

———◆———

I was as mad as a three-legged dog trying to bury a turd on an icy pond.

———◆———

It's harder than trying to stick a wet noodle in a wildcat's ass.

———◆———

Even a dog knows the difference between being stumbled over and kicked.

———◆———

I'M PROUDER OF THAT THAN A HOUND PUP IS HIS FIRST FLEA.

He's shiverin' like a dog tryin'
to shit a peach seed.

HE'S SO CROSS-EYED HE CAN STAND
ON THE FRONT PORCH AND COUNT
CHICKENS IN THE BACKYARD.

Whiter than a hound dog's tooth.

IT'S HARD TO FLY WITH THE
EAGLES WHEN YOU RUN
AROUND WITH THE TURKEYS.

Quieter than a mouse peeing on cotton.

He's so lazy he calls the dog in to see if it's rainin'.

Ain't no point in beatin' a dead horse— 'course, can't hurt none either.

He's all hat and no cattle.

Smooth as a pig on stilts.

RICHER THAN THREE FEET UP A BULL'S ASS.

You're as handy as a cow on crutches.

MORE FUN THAN A SACKFUL OF KITTENS AND A LUMP HAMMER.

It smelled worse than a dead skunk that just crawled out of another dead skunk's ass.

Flashy as a rat with a gold tooth.
(not to be trusted)

LIKE FINDIN' A FEATHER ON A FROG.

That dog won't hunt.

That's like findin' a diamond in a billy goat's ass.

BEATIN' A DEAD HORSE DON'T MAKE IT TASTE BETTER.

I'm busier than a borrowed mule.

It's so dry, the trees are bribing the dogs.

You couldn't get laid in a monkey whorehouse if you had a bushel of bananas.

———◆———

My cow died last night, so I don't need your bull.

———◆———

He's more confused than a turtle on the center stripe.

———◆———

TROUBLE WITH A MILK COW IS SHE WON'T STAY MILKED.

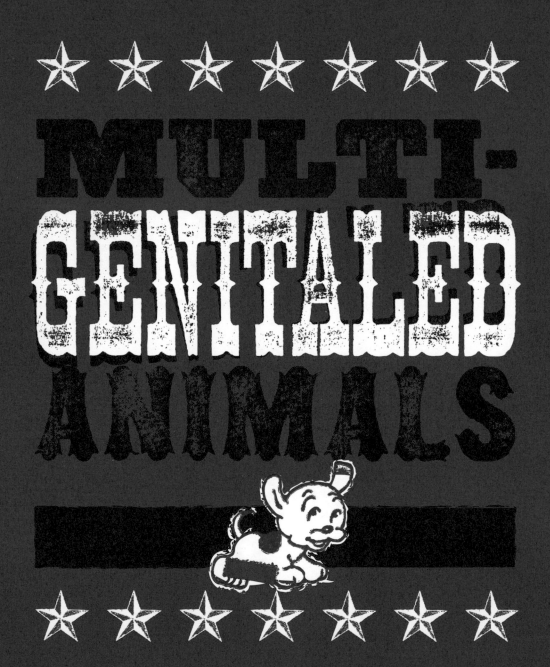

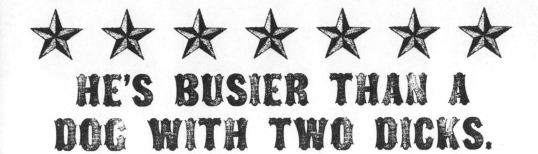

HE'S BUSIER THAN A DOG WITH TWO DICKS.

Hornier than a twelve-peckered billy goat in mating season.

Hotter than a three-balled tomcat.

HAPPIER THAN A PUPPY WITH TWO PETERS.

It's rainin' harder than a double–cunted cow pissin' on a flat rock.

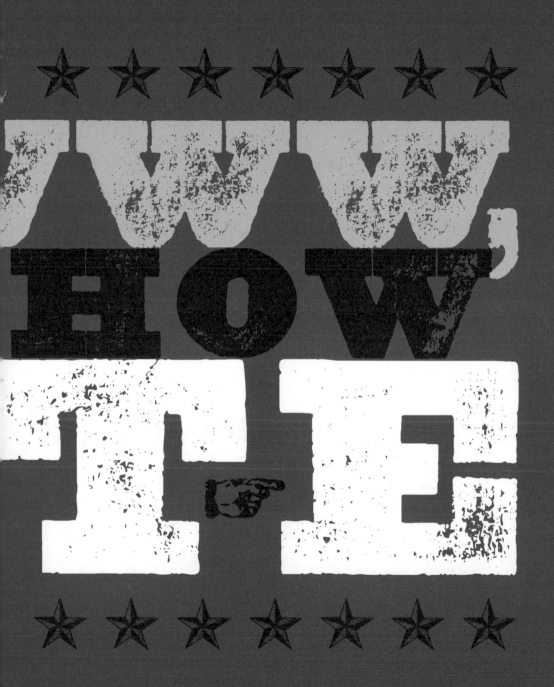

She's purtier than a mess of fried catfish.

CUTER THAN A LITTLE OL' BALL OF COTTON ROLLIN' UNDER A BARBED-WIRE FENCE.

She's like a twelve-pound bass: you don't know whether to eat her or mount her.

She's cuter than pig nipples.

She's as pretty as a new set of snow tires.

Prettier than a wall full of boogers in the men's bathroom.

❧

She's so fine, I'd crawl through a minefield of broken glass on my hands and knees to hear her piss in a tin can over a walkie-talkie.

❧

YOU'RE FINER 'N FROG HAIR SPLIT EIGHT WAYS.

❧

PRETTIER THAN A SPECKLED PUP UNDER A WAGON WITH HIS TONGUE HANGIN' OUT.

❧

Cute as a sackful o' puppies.

If you buy that, you might as well shove your money
up a wolf's ass and watch him run over the hill.

· · · · · · · · ·

DON'T LET THE DOOR HIT YA WHERE THE GOOD LORD SPLIT YA.

· · · · · · · · ·

SWAT MY HIND WITH A MELON RIND.

· · · · · · · · ·

His ass must be hungry—it's tryin' to eat his pants.

· · · · · · · · ·

The only thing fair is the hair on
a Norwegian albino's butt.

· · · · · · · · ·

IF HE RAN UP YOUR ASS WITH TRACK
SHOES ON, YOU'D KNOW WHERE HE'S AT.

· · · · · · · · ·

He ran like his feet was on fire
and his butt was catchin'.

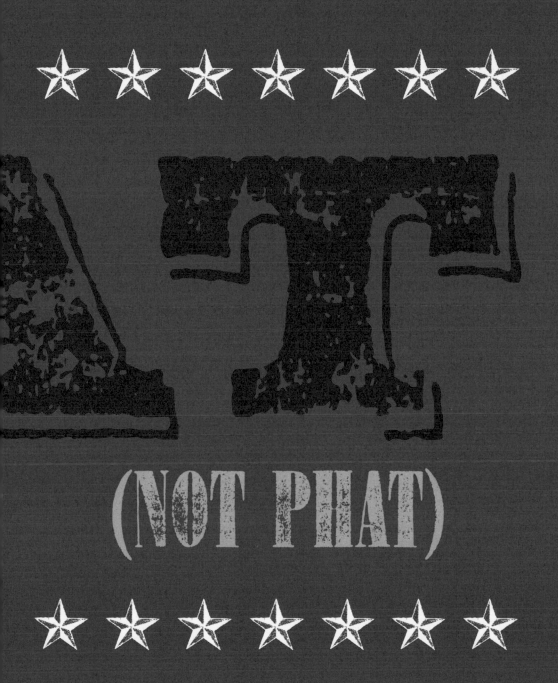

He looks like three pounds of ugly in a two-pound sack.

Drivin' a Dodge truck is like doin' a fat gal: ya ain't real proud of it, but it works.

She had a butt like a forty-dollar mule.

Fat people are harder to kidnap.

That goes through more batteries than a lonely fat girl on a Saturday night.

He's got the furniture disease:
his chest done fell into his drawers.

I ain't no Barbie, but I ain't
big enough to eat hay.

She's so fat, if somebody told her to
"haul ass," she'd have to make two trips.

I'M OUT LIKE A FAT
KID IN DODGEBALL.

Her ass was so big, it looked like two
Buicks fighting for a parking place.

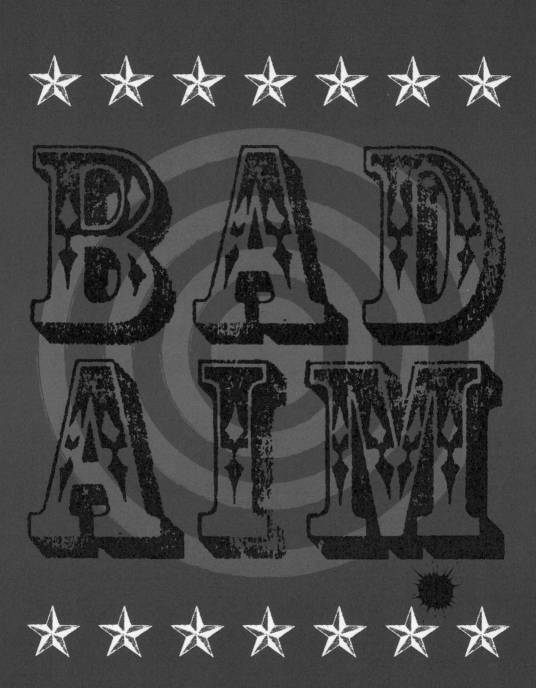

He couldn't hit water if he
was standin' on a boat.

HE COULDN'T HIT THE BROAD SIDE OF A BARN.

He couldn't hit a ten-point buck with a
twelve-gauge one yard in front of him.

*He couldn't hit a bull in the
butt with a bucket of rice.*

HE COULDN'T HIT A BULL IN THE BUTT WITH A BASS FIDDLE.

STUPID
IS AS

STUPID DOES

YOUR PARENTS MUSTA' PISSED IN A POT AND RAISED A BLOOMIN' IDIOT.

That boy ain't smart enough to pound sand in a rat hole.

You could fuck up an anvil with a rubber mallet.

He's duller than a three-watt light bulb in a power outage.

It's kinda like puttin' gas in a car that you've already wrecked.

He was so confused he didn't know his ass from his elbow.

You're as smart as you are good lookin', and that ain't sayin' much.

If brains was cotton you wouldn't have enough to Kotex a flea.

He's so dumb, he couldn't spell *cat* if you spotted him the C and the T.

———◆———

He's so stupid, he thinks Johnny Cash is a pay toilet.

———◆———

She's a taco shy of a combination plate.

———◆———

He's so stupid they had to burn down the school just to get him out of the third grade.

———◆———

HE AIN'T THE BRIGHTEST CRAYON IN THE BOX.

———◆———

THAT BOY DON'T KNOW SHEEP SHIT FROM ARBUCKLE COFFEE.

———◆———

You're about as stupid as an ass-roaming butt monkey.

———◆———

DUMBER THAN A BOX OF DIRT.

She's dumb as a brick.

A few fries short of a Happy Meal.

He's so dumb he couldn't pour piss out of a boot if the instructions was written on the heel.

That boy ain't got the sense to wipe hisself when he's done.

THAT BOY'S DUMBER THAN A STICK OF WOOD.

He's so dumb he couldn't get into college with a crowbar.

That boy is nine dimes short of a dollar.

Puttin' her brain in a matchbox would be like a BB rollin' around in a boxcar.

Sometimes I think that girl is as dumb as a cat tryin' to look pretty in the middle of a dog festival.

HE AIN'T GOT THE SENSE TO LEAD A BLIND GOOSE TO SHIT.

That man don't have the brains God graced a bale of hay.

He's got all the smarts God gave a duck's ass.

Dumber than a bag of hammers.

That boy's so stupid he took a duck to a chicken fight.

That boy is about as sharp as a cue ball.

He's so stupid, he couldn't find his ass with both hands.

You don't know your ass from apple butter.

He's a beer short of a six-pack.

HE COULDN'T HIT HIS OWN ASS WITH DIRECTIONS AND A MAP.

He ain't the sharpest knife in the drawer.

He don't know "come here" from "sic 'em."

She was so dumb that she thought GrapeNuts was a venereal disease and Peter Pan was a hospital utensil.

He's a few sandwiches short of a picnic.

If brains was dynamite, she wouldn't have enough to blow her nose.

He couldn't find his ass with two hands and a flashlight.

Dumber than a box of rocks.

Plumb eat up with the dumb-ass.

You'd mess up a wet dream.

If brains was lard, you couldn't grease too big a wheel.

THAT MAKES ABOUT AS MUCH SENSE AS A SCREEN DOOR ON A SUBMARINE.

Busier than ants at a picnic.

BUSIER THAN A SET OF JUMPER CABLES AT A MEXICAN FUNERAL.

Busier than a one–armed man in a fistfight.

Busier than a tick on a cat's back.

BUSIER THAN A STUMP FULL OF ANTS.

Busier than a one–armed paper hanger.

I got more things to do than a dog with fleas.

Busier than a cat tryin' to
cover crap on a marble floor.

★ ★ ★ ★ ★ ★ ★

CAN'T LIVE WITH 'EM,

★ ★ ★ ★ ★ ★ ★

CAN'T SHOOT 'EM

Women have to be more beautiful than smart, 'cause men see better than they think.

———◆———

Women are like tiles: you lay 'em right the first time, they let you walk all over 'em for life.

———◆———

IT TAKES A WHOLE LOTTA LIQUOR TO LIKE 'ER.

———◆———

SHE DIDN'T GET A ROUND MOUTH BY EATIN' SQUARE MEALS.

She looks like she was rode rough
and put away wet.

IT MUST BE JELLY, 'CAUSE
JAM DON'T SHAKE LIKE THAT.

She's a carpenter's dream:
flat as a board and ain't
never been nailed.

Sadder than a fat girl
with no boobs.

*She's as wild as a
peach orchard boar.*

MARRIAGE IS AN EXPENSIVE WAY FOR A MAN TO GET HIS LAUNDRY DONE FOR FREE.

HER ASS LOOKED LIKE TWO PIGS IN A GUNNYSACK.

She's built like a brick shithouse.

Sex with her is like throwin' a hot dog down a hallway.

She's got her nose stuck up so high
in the air she'd drown if it rained.

✦— ❈ —✦

She got her tit caught
in a wringer.

✦— ❈ —✦

**She's limber
as a dishrag.**

✦— ❈ —✦

**HER TEETH ARE LIKE STARS:
THEY COME OUT AT NIGHT.**

✦— ❈ —✦

She's been takin' them
"noassatall pills."

It's colder than a witch's titty on a winter day on the shady side of the mountain.

COLDER THAN A MOTHER-IN-LAW'S LOVE.

It's colder than a witch's titty in a brass bra doin' push-ups in the snow.

It's colder than a well digger's ass in Idaho.

It's colder than a witch's titty facedown in the snow with a Popsicle shoved up her ass.

IT'S COLDER THAN A BRASS TOILET SEAT ON THE SHADY SIDE OF AN ICEBERG.

Crazier than a dog in a hubcap factory.

He's crazier than a shithouse fly.

NUTTIER THAN A FIVE-POUND FRUITCAKE.

That kid is nuttier than a pecan pie!

NUTTIER THAN A SQUIRREL TURD.

HE'S CRAZY AS A PIG EATIN' SHIT.

LOOPY AS A CROSS-EYED COWPOKE'S LARIAT.

NUTTIER THAN A PORT-O-POTTY AT A PEANUT FESTIVAL.

IT'S GETTIN'

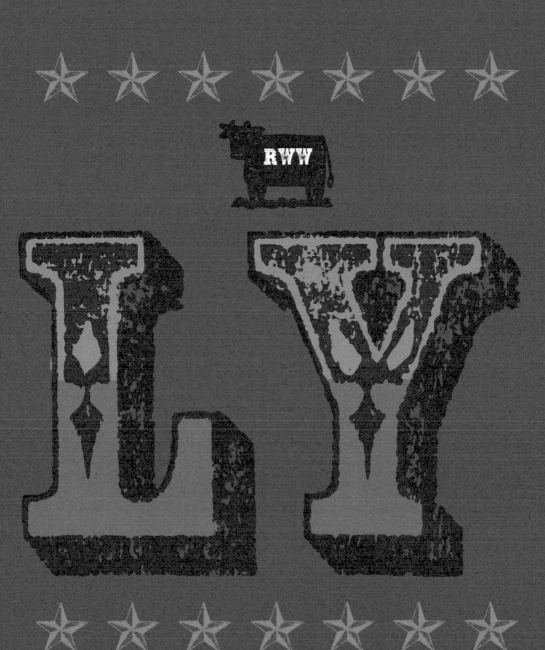

She looks like she got hit in the face with a bag of what-the-fuck.

***

LAST TIME I SAW A MOUTH LIKE THAT IT HAD A BIT IN IT.

***

She's so ugly she'd knock a buzzard off a gut wagon.

***

Ugly as three miles of mud road.

***

He's so bucktoothed he could eat corn on the cob through a picket fence.

SHE'S SO UGLY SHE COULD STOP A BUCKET OF SNOT IN MID-AIR.

That's about as ugly as Uncle Bob's divorce.

HE'S UGLIER THAN MY GRANDDADDY'S BEER BELLY AT A REDNECK WEDDING.

ONLY THING ALIVE AT THAT HOUSE WITH ALL ITS TEETH IS THE TERMITES.

She's uglier than a hat full of assholes.

She's so ugly she could stop a clock.

IF YOU FELL INTO A POND, YOU COULD SKIM OFF UGLY FOR A WEEK.

She's so ugly, she looks like she plays goalie for a dart team.

She's uglier than a mud fence.

She's so ugly, she could scare a rat off a cheesecake.

He's uglier than a bucket of assholes with the best ones picked out.

She's uglier than a mole on a pig's ass.

THAT GIRL IS AS UGLY AS HOMEMADE SOAP.

Is that your head or did your neck throw up?

She's so ugly, we had to tie a pork chop around her neck to get the dogs to play with her.

She looks like she got hit in the face with a sackful of bent nickels.

You must have fell from a ugly tree
and hit every branch coming down.

She was so ugly she looked like her
face had caught fire and someone beat
it out with a track shoe.

**She's so ugly she'd make a
freight train take a dirt road.**

She looks like she got shot
in the face with rock salt.

UGLIER THAN A BAG OF DICKS.

She's so ugly, she looks like she ran a forty-yard dash in a thirty-yard gym.

UGLIER THAN A BUCKET FULL OF ARMPITS.

Somebody ruined a perfectly good asshole when they put teeth in your mouth.

She's about as pretty as a speckled pup's butt.

She looks like her face caught fire and somebody put it out with an ice pick.

GEORGIA ON

MY MIND

IT'S HOTTER THAN HELL AND HALF OF GEORGIA.

I'LL SKIN YOU LIKE A GEORGIA CATFISH.

HE WENT THROUGH THAT LIKE SHERMAN WENT THROUGH GEORGIA.

IT'S HOTTER THAN GEORGIA ASPHALT.

83

NOT JUST GOOD

That food tastes so good it makes you wanna slap your grandma.

So good, it'll make your tongue jump out and lick the eyebrows right off your head.

I ain't as good as I once was, but I'm better once than I ever was.

Gooder 'n snuff and ain't half as dusty.

THAT FOOD IS SO GOOD IT MAKES YOUR TONGUE BEAT A HOLE IN THE ROOF OF YOUR MOUTH AND SLAP YOUR BRAIN.

That tastes so good, if you put it on your head, your tongue would slap your face tryin' to get to it.

HOW'S BUSINESS? GOOD ENOUGH FOR CORK WINE.

This stuff will put a freeze on your face that won't quit.
(refers to good moonshine)

That adhesive's so good, it'd hold a bad marriage together.

IT'S SO GOOD, IT'LL MAKE YA PUT BACK SHIT YOU DIDN'T EVEN STEAL.

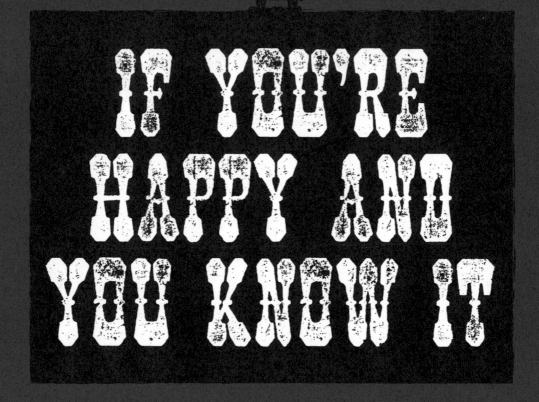

IF YOU'RE
HAPPY AND
YOU KNOW IT

Happier than a pig in shit.

HAPPIER THAN A POSSUM IN THE CORNCRIB WITH THE DOG TIED UP.

Smilin' like a possum eatin' fish.

HE'S AS HAPPY AS A FAT GUY AT THE BUFFET.

Happier than a june bug on a tomato plant.

I'm happy as a jackass in a briar patch.

It's so hot you could sweat 150 pounds of fat off a 125-pound hog.

IT'S HOTTER THAN A BLISTERED DICK IN A WOOL SOCK.

Hotter than a whore in church.

It's hotter than the Devil's underarm.

IT'S HOTTER THAN A TWO-DOLLAR PISTOL.

It's hotter than a Wal-Mart parking lot in August.

It's wipe-your-ass-with-a-snow-cone hot.

Hotter than a two-dollar whore on dollar day.

It's hotter than forty acres of burnin' stumps.

IT'S HOTTER THAN A GOAT'S ASS IN A PEPPER PATCH.

HOT AS A DEPOT STOVE.

It's so hot, I seen a coyote chasin' a jackrabbit, and they's both walkin'.

Hotter than a road lizard walking up a hill backwards carryin' a bucket of feed.

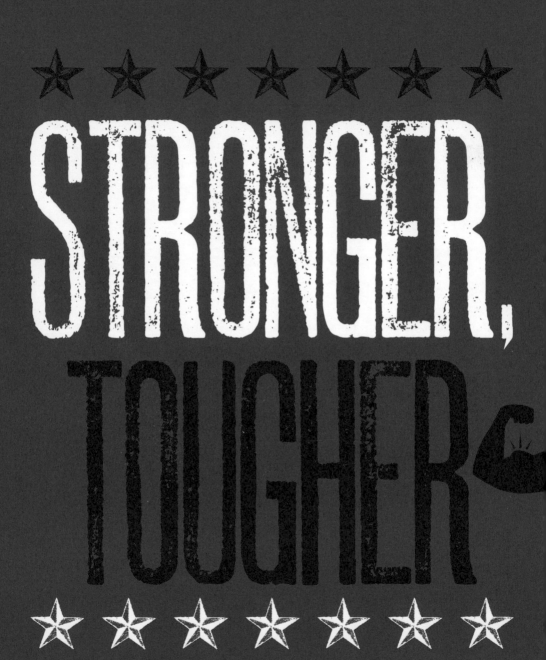

STRONGER THAN TEN ACRES OF GARLIC.

· · · · · · ·

Like a garlic milkshake: smooth, yet strong.

· · · · · · ·

Strong as train smoke.

· · · · · ·

THAT GUY'S GOT MORE GUTS THAN A MAN CAN HANG ON A FENCE.

· · · · · · ·

STRONG AS BEAR'S BREATH.

· · · · · · ·

Tougher than a two-dollar steak.

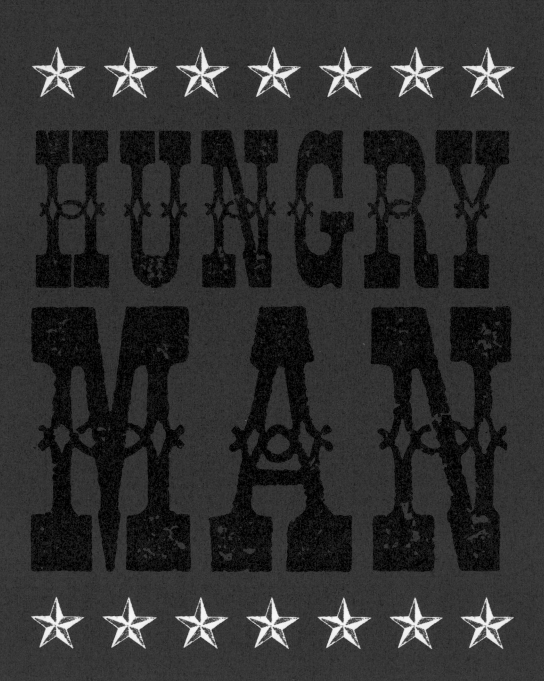

I'M SO HUNGRY MY BACKBONE IS SNAPPIN' AT MY BELT BUCKLE.

I'm so hungry I'd eat the balls off a low-flyin' duck.

I'M HUNGRY AS A CUT-SHOT DOG!

I'm as hungry as a tick on a turnip.

I'M SO HUNGRY I COULD EAT THE ASS OUT OF A ROADKILL ARMADILLO.

I'm so hungry I could eat the asshole out of a skunk.

I'M SO HUNGRY I COULD EAT THE NORTH END OF A COW GOIN' SOUTH.

 not me  RWW

I'D

RATHER

I'd rather WEAR A PAIR OF PORKCHOP PANTIES AND RUN THROUGH A LION'S DEN THAN...

I'd rather SLIDE DOWN A MOUNTAIN OF RAZOR BLADES AND JUMP INTO A POOL OF RUBBING ALCOHOL THAN...

I'd rather JUMP BAREFOOT OFF A SIX-FOOT STEPLADDER INTO A FIVE-GALLON BUCKET OF PORCUPINES THAN...

MAD MAD WORLD

I'm madder than a deaf person trying to play bingo, get bingo, and holler out bingo.

Boy, you just done pissed me off. You better start runnin' like your head's on fire and your ass is catchin'.

Madder than a legless Ethiopian watchin' a donut roll down a hill.

Madder than a long-tail cat in a room full of rockin' chairs.

He's madder than a puffed toad.

She's madder than a bobcat caught in a piss fire.

I'm so mad I could just fall out of my pants.

That's enough to piss the pope off!

MADDER THAN AN AMISH ELECTRICIAN.

Madder than Janet Reno's blind date.

BETTER PISSED OFF THAN PISSED ON.

Mad as a box of frogs.

I'm so mad I could swallow gunpowder, two bullets, eat a burrito, take off my britches, lay on my back, spread my ass cheeks, fart, and drop a deer from a hundred yards.

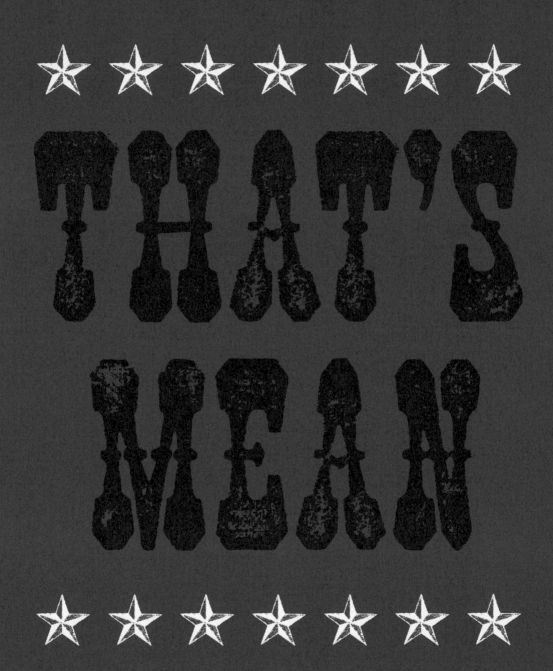

MEANER THAN AN OLD WET HEN.

Mean as the alligator when
the pond went dry.

MEANNESS DON'T JUST HAPPEN OVERNIGHT.

Don't corner somethin' that you
know is meaner than you.

He's so mean, he wouldn't give his mother the sweat off his balls.

MEASURE
TWICE

CUT ONCE

Lower than an ankle bracelet on a flat-footed pigmy.

THINNER THAN A GNAT'S SCROTUM STRETCHED OVER A FIFTY-FIVE-GALLON DRUM.

Quick as a politician's promise.

I'm so poor I can't pay attention.

WE'RE TRADIN' DAYLIGHT FOR DARK.

As scarce as hens' teeth.

THAT AIN'T WORTH THE POWDER TO BLOW IT TO HELL.

Tighter than fish pussy
(and that shit is watertight).

I ain't goin' no higher than corn and no lower than taters.

I'M DOIN' AS LITTLE AS POSSIBLE AND THE EASY ONES TWICE.

Smaller than a skeeter peter.

I'm as dry as a nun's nasty.

You're gonna catch nine shades of hell.

NOISIER THAN TWO SKELETONS SCREWING ON A TIN ROOF.

I hope it rains ass-high to an eight-foot Indian.

Thinner than a skeeter's ass stretched over a wash tub.

FINER THAN A FROG'S HAIR.

Tighter than Dick's hatband.

THAT'S ABOUT AS MUCH FUN AS A BAD CASE OF SCOURS.

That guy's harder to catch than my wife's boyfriend.

MORE FUCKED UP THAN A CAN OF FISHHOOKS.

THAT'LL SPIN FASTER THAN THE HANDLE ON A SHITHOUSE DOOR.

I feel lower than a bow-legged caterpillar.

Tighter than a tick.

Slower than a herd of turtles stampedin' through peanut butter.

Tighter than a skeeter's ass in a nosedive.

TIGHTER THAN A BULL'S ASS DURING FLY SEASON.

HARDER THAN A BLIND LESBIAN'S NIPPLES AT A FISH MARKET.

Sober as a judge.

THAT'S LOWER THAN WHALE SHIT, AND THAT'S AT THE BOTTOM OF THE SEA.

Country fences need to be horse high, pig tight, and bull strong.

A BUMBLEBEE IS FASTER THAN A JOHN DEERE TRACTOR.

Tighter than a rat's ass in a keyhole.

Thicker than the hair on a rabbit's back.

That room's so small you can't cuss a cat without gettin' a mouthful of fur.

ALL WORKED UP

Wound up tighter than a two-dollar watch.

She's wound up tighter than the girdle
of a Baptist minister's wife at an
all-you-can-eat pancake breakfast.

NERVOUS AS A BEAR CAUGHT

★ ★ ★ ★ ★ ★ ★ ★ ★ ★ ★ ★ ★ ★ ★

WITH HIS HEAD IN THE HIVE.

That guy's so nervous you couldn't drive a
needle up his ass with a jackhammer.

Nervous as a jerked-off cat.

117

That fella is thick in the middle and poor on both ends.

I COULDN'T GET NAILED IN A WOOD WORKSHOP.

You could dive into a barrel of tits and come out suckin' your thumb.

SHE'D SOONER CLIMB A TREE TO TELL A LIE THAN STAND ON THE GROUND AND TELL THE TRUTH.

Son, you're so low that when you die you're gonna have to rise up to find hell.

✦

He'd steal the bridle off a nightmare.

✦

You lie like a tombstone.

✦

HE RAN LIKE A SCALDED DOG.

✦

Boy, you could fuck up a mother's love.

✦

You're so sorry, you'd steal a widow woman's dog.

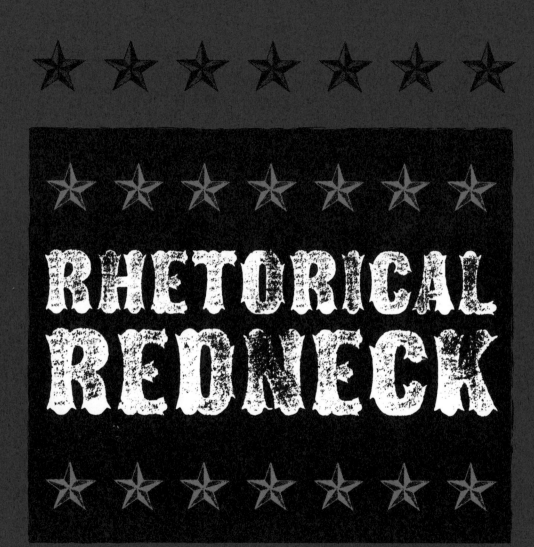

RHETORICAL REDNECK

DOES A BEAR SHIT IN THE WOODS?

IS A FROG'S ASS WATERTIGHT?

DOES A FAT DOG FART?

DOES HOWDY DOODY HAVE WOODEN BALLS?

IS THE POPE CATHOLIC?

PISS SHIT
(AND OTHER RELATED AREAS)

I'm on you like stink on shit.

He's feelin' lower than a turd in the gutter with the shit kicked out of it.

I feel like I was shot at and missed, shit at and hit.

BOY, I'LL SLAP A FART OUTTA YOU THAT'LL WHISTLE LIKE A FREIGHT TRAIN!

I'M GONNA BE LIKE SHIT AND HIT THE TRAIL.

If you stir shit long enough, you'll get some on you.

You can put a coat and tie on a turd but it's still gonna be a turd.

THE ONLY THING WE GOT TO FEAR IS A PUBLIC TOILET SEAT.

If I wanted shit, I'd squeeze your head.

I smell what you're steppin' in.
("I get it.")

That looks like shit on a white rabbit.

Subtle as an unflushed toilet.

It's like wipin' your ass with a hula hoop: it goes round 'n' round with no end to it and you only get shit on.

What's the matter? Got a turd crossways?

Well shit on me and call me a sundae!

THAT FART SMELLED LIKE IT CRAWLED OVER A TURD TO GET OUT.

That'll go over like a fart in church.

I wouldn't piss on him if his guts was on fire.

Shit the bed then kick it out!

SHIT FIRE AND SAVE A MATCH.

Slower than smoke rollin' off of dog shit in December.

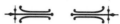

I feel like I got eat by a bear and shit off a cliff.

THIS KNIFE IS SO DULL, IT WOULDN'T CUT A FART.

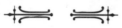

THAT'LL GO OVER LIKE A TURD IN A PUNCH BOWL.

Don't pee down my back and tell me it's rainin'.

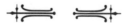

I gotta piss like a pregnant woman.

The closest you ever came to gettin' a piece of ass was when your finger tore through the toilet paper.

Well, don't that just beat all ya ever stepped in.

That's like wipin' before ya poop. It don't make no sense.

We thought we were shittin' in high cotton.
(feeling pretty special)

I got a bad case of the zacklies: my mouth tastes zackly like my butt smells.

I got to piss like a rushin' racehorse.

It's time to piss on the campfire and call the dogs.

If you shake it more than three times, you're playin' with it.

Rare as rocking-horse shit.

LIFE IS LIKE A SHIT SANDWICH. THE MORE BREAD YOU HAVE, THE LESS SHIT YOU HAVE TO EAT.

YOU CAN'T POLISH A TURD.

I'M SO TOUGH, MY TURDS HAVE MUSCLES ON 'EM.

FOOD FOR THOUGHT

He's ridin' a gravy train on biscuit wheels.

Her cookin's so bad, you couldn't poke a fork through the gravy.

You catch more flies with jam than you do with vinegar.

This knife is so dull it wouldn't cut hot butter.

YOU CAN CATCH MORE FLIES WITH HONEY, BUT WHO WANTS FLIES?

That piano player's fingers are slipperier than sausage on a griddle.

You're slower than molasses on a cold day.

Well, butter my butt and call me a biscuit!

SHE WOULDN'T WALK ACROSS THE STREET TO SEE A PISS-ANT EAT A BALE OF HAY.

He's scratched up worse than a blind berry picker.

IF YOU KEEP STEALIN' OUR FARMLAND, WE'LL ALL BE EATIN' CHINESE.

Ain't no thing but a chicken wing.

He's as country as cornflakes.

I'm just hangin' out like a hair in a biscuit!

SHE'S AS USEFUL AS A TIT ON A BOAR HOG.

He ain't exactly settin' the woods on fire. (is lazy)

ABOUT AS USEFUL AS BUTTONS ON A DISHRAG.

Useful as balls on a priest.

You're as useful as a ball in a square dance.

I'LL HIT YOU SO HARD YOUR WHOLE FAMILY WILL HURT!

IF YOU'RE GONNA BE STUPID, YOU BETTER BE TOUGH.

BOY, I'LL SMACK YOU SO HARD YOUR KIDS'LL COME OUT BEHAVIN'.

DON'T MAKE ME OPEN UP A CAN O' WHUP ASS!

You got a can o' whup ass? Bring it over, 'cause I have the can opener.

I'll knock a knot on your head so tall you'll have to climb a ladder to comb your hair.

I'm gonna put a knot in your head the Boy Scouts can't get out.

I'm gonna slap you like a red-headed stepchild.

I'm gonna kick your ass so hard you'll have to take your shirt off to shit.

KEEP MESSIN' WITH ME AND I'LL STOMP A MUDHOLE IN YOUR ASS AND WALK IT DRY.

I'M GONNA KICK YOUR ASS TILL IT HUMS LIKE A TENPENNY FINISHIN' NAIL HIT WITH A GREASY BALL-PEEN HAMMER.

You'd rather jack off a grizzly bear with a fistful of cockleburs than to fuck with me.

YOU COULDN'T SCRATCH MY ASS IF YOU WAS A MOUNTAIN LION.

I wouldn't piss in your mouth if your teeth was on fire.

I don't play—I quit school 'cause of recess.

If you can't hang with the big dogs, stay your puppy ass on the porch!

I'M GONNA BEAT YOU SENSELESS AND TELL GOD YOU WAS DRUG BY A HORSE.

I'm sorry, but my tongue got in front of my eyetooth and I couldn't see what I was saying.

Well, throw me between an axle housing and frame and call me shocked!

RUNS JUST LIKE A CANDLE.

YOU LIE LIKE A CHEAP RUG.

HE'S DEAF IN ONE EAR AND CAN'T HEAR OUT OF THE OTHER.

Let's put some lipstick on this pig!

★ ★ ★ ★ ★ ★ ★ ★ ★ ★ ★
ACKNOWLEDGMENTS

Thank you to everyone who has contributed words of wisdom to this project (and keep 'em coming).

I would also like to thank the following for their help, support, and inspiration: Jessica, Josie, Stella, and Milo Muehlhausen; Sarah Malarkey; Pat Hawk (the least redneck person I know); Steve Hawk; Tony Hawk; Mike Hawkins; Roger Sgarbossa; Jim Muehlhausen; Jill, Peter, Jenna, and Carter Linsley; Marie and Timmy and the entire South Carolina family; Bob and Ellen and the Virginia family; Randy Laybourne; Rob Quillen; Dave Quillen; Greg E. Noll; David Anderson (a redneck in hiding); Rob Campbell; Kenny Rogers; Charlize Theron; Chanel Bohn; Contusion Design; Fender Guitars; the Walden Font Company; everyone at THI except Jerome; and everyone at Chronicle Books.

"We ain't much, but we're all we got."

REDNECK WORDS OF WISDOM

RWW